FRENCH RESTAURANT

A Poetry Collection

Renee de la Roche-Zhu

Liminal Press

Copyright © 2024 Renee de la Roche-Zhu

All rights reserved

Revised Edition © 2025 Renee de la Roche-Zhu

This revised version of French Restaurant includes minor updates to the content and design. Some poems from the original publication have been removed for coherence. This version remains under the original ISBN.

The characters and events portrayed in this book are fictitious. Any similarity to real persons, living or dead, is coincidental and not intended by the author.

No part of this book may be reproduced, or stored in a retrieval system, or transmitted in any form or by any means, electronic, mechanical, photocopying, recording, or otherwise, without express written permission of the publisher.

ISBN-13: 979-8-218-38194-3

Printed in the United States of America

To my friends, to my family - you know who you are. To myself, you now know who you are.

INTRODUCTION

I never intended for *French Restaurant* to be just a poetry collection. I wanted it to be a chronicle of my turbulent twenties spanning different continents, weaving the quotidian with the philosophical. I also wanted it to reflect the lessons I wish I'd learned earlier in life that could be relevant for young people, especially young women, navigating the tumult of their twenties and early thirties.

In 2019, I began formally writing poetry when I moved from New York City to Tokyo, which started with a brief international consulting stint in Hong Kong. This period of upheaval was marked by both exciting encounters with people from drastically different walks of life and atomized feelings of isolation and otherness, the latter persisted upon my return to New York amidst the pandemic. Along the way, I also made meaningful stops in London, Paris, Toronto, etc.

In telling stories that took place in these various cities, my poetry also grapples with the contingent and relational nature of identity (à la Foucault) and in particular what it means to be a woman (De Beauvoir), the genealogies of power structures (Nietzsche) in modern societies, the shifting and liminal nature of existence and reality (Satre, Hegel), and the search for meaning (Kierkegaard) informed by individual choice and authenticity.

While I am deeply interested in elevating the quotidian to philosophical altitudes, I am primarily motivated by the richness of the everyday, both the big and the small – a dying romance in Tokyo, making new memories with an old friend, the fluorescent lights in a meeting room, making chia pudding in the kitchen, career highs and setbacks, etc. In some poems, the philosophical poses a question, to which the quotidian serves up an answer – while in others, it is the other way around.

Finally, this collection also encapsulates some learnings I wish I'd grasped earlier in life. For instance, in the eponymous poem "French Restaurant", readers are, hopefully, encouraged to savor moments of community and camaraderie, echoing Michelle Obama's sentiment of nurturing one's 'Kitchen Table' in her work *The Light We Carry*, rather than allowing the eagerness for a new potential romance (oftentimes with strangers) to overshadow the opportunity for genuine communal connection.

As you linger in the ethereal, liminal space of a "French Restaurant" set against Martian landscapes, I hope these verses evoke feelings of joy, belonging, and nostalgia, reminiscent of the cherished moments shared with loved ones at your favorite French restaurant on Earth.

CONTENTS

Title Page
Copyright
Dedication
Introduction
Chapter 1: New York   1
Chapter 2: Tokyo   43
Chapter 3: London   53
Chapter 4: Hong Kong   62
Chapter 5: Paris, Rome, Zermatt, Tasmania, Toronto   67
Chapter 6: California & Arizona   74
Afterword   79
About The Author   81

CHAPTER 1: NEW YORK

French Restaurant

Back in New York, I think I fractured your light
Once upon a story
It refracted and echoed down the city streets
Arched like a cat –
Once waiting for Life, past and
Present
Life that tells us what we want. Yet now the future
Can't arrive fast enough
I draw in the photons as they hasten
I feel my twenties passing through me like a breeze
I feel it passing
Ceaselessly

Out of the kernel of darkness I sprang
From the hard-boiled edge of this world
Towards words of alternate eventualities
Hungered for the colossus of Hunter S. Thompson
To die at my hands
Arrogance – it pinches my nerves
I once told you
At the height of our cynicism
They are
Lampshades made of black onyx

FRENCH RESTAURANT

Sagging in zero gravity, not even
Thirty

Sometimes aboard a spaceship I notice
The violence of the blue sunset mantling the horizon –
In these moments I pause
To think of Earth
And of you
In flashes
We were not yet twenty-four
We were pre-World War III
We were rising like the October moon on your
Roof
Young enough then to know
Everything

In this blinding light I breathe and remember everything:
I see you, beckoning to me about a silly
Study or a dinner
French restaurant
The food is less than memorable
But we swirl in elation with those around us
You talk to me with a sweeter solace than the 'date' I leave for subsequently
From this vantage point I feel the moment and its enormity

Its timeless eyes
The cosmos glides past me
This time, we never stop being
Happy

Days On Mars

Along the sea, by the beach
Do you contemplate me –
And what's at the heart of things – is a question I don't need
Answers to; for I know you do
I have seen the likeness of you in ancient cave paintings
But when all the water evaporates, are these our last or first days on Mars?

Life here takes place at pace as I go to the farmers markets
On Saturdays. Still, the nights are cursed with two moons
When my darkness surges and the Martian storm takes you in –
Run the laundry machine, eat a piece of tea cake, and wait for it to end
On the journey here it looked like I've decorated the storyboard with the big questions: The future of humanity –
But I'm consumed by the palpable fragilities of our life, here and back home

Somewhere else in spacetime, my father is a family man – in the front seat

Of his car, he asks me 'what would you like to eat'

As we drive towards Mercury; he turns up the radio, and asks me

To listen to the sound of a supermassive blackhole – 'do you hear Him?'

And I say, 'oh'. He says, 'I know'

No one awaits us at home except a singularity

The light fades into my bedroom, two sixteen

Dreams embody me – I travel in waves of subconsciousness, foaming

Towards yellow-collared orange tulips

But will there be safety on this sterile planet in each of the ways I exist and breathe

Will you learn to paint every fragment of me and my being

Of my heart expanding, as time does, over the surface of an insensate galaxy

FRENCH RESTAURANT

ザ・プリンスギャラリ
À La Anne Sexton

(Prince Gallery Hotel,
À La Anne Sexton)

In my dream, sinking into the blue marrow
of the skeleton of my colossus
My real, unimpeded dream
I'm running up and down Kioicho-dori
In sweat I search for a street sign
that hangs above the river at the Prince Hotel
"Jazz here tonight, Black & white moonshine"

I walk in a yellow dress on Bleecker Street
And a black pocketbook filled with makeup,
enough excuses, my work phone, and wallet
And on the edge of twenty-five, or is it forty-five
I pace, I pace
I hold up matches at street signs
For I've crossed a line

I have lost my orange typewriter

And a father who has wiped off his eyes
In order to take me at my surface curvature
Walking, and looking, and walking again – this is not a dream
Just my life
Where I'm running out of alibis
And the hotel is unfindable for a lifetime

I open my black pocketbook
As women do
And sharks swim between the dollars and lipstick,
and between the dead skull of the miserly & shallow man I once lay my head next to
And the good men for whom I put the killer in me to sleep in front of a glass mirror
In my life I live
In the waves I stay asleep, but breathe

Note: Written in honor of Anne Sexton's "45 Mercy Street"

A Woman Is A Woman

July it is again – clouds gather on my mind
And in the lathering thickness of my matcha latte
In West Village summer tourists frolic amongst vapid insta-thots
And third-rate marketing professionals
As Bleecker Street flows downtown, reeking like an incandescent river of dross

It's hard not to ask – but what has the Village
Done to itself? And what have I
Done to myself? I've lost my special edition dark sunglasses
After the cleaning lady came last week – but did I also the two years
Whilst I've had them since I came back from Tokyo?

On the sixtieth-something floor of WTC a few aggressive men ask me
Questions they do not want real answers to
Anger and condescension line my black pockets
They seek to arbitrate the rights of my voice, and my body eventually –
My procession to the grave

In my closet my dresses stay up all night conversing with my trousers
Not knowing I can hear everything – the soundtrack of my
Extinction if I stay put. The grey veins of the Moon – running within which not blood
But detergent
I wait for a complete statement of my actions

This is what living hell feels like – this waiting after you'd been passed over
It feels and tastes like chalk powder, irritating your throat
The uncertainty of death hangs upon my bedframe and looks at me with a casual eye
The banality and ugliness of vacuous men suffocate me
On this dead leaf of a street I'm a woman shark out of water

It Was Later Than I Thought

In my days at 123 Washington silence grows
Like vines, with fortitude and a solemn numbness in equal measure
Next to these crisp windows it swallows me completely
For the sun comes up every day, but is it only a habit, like love
My heart, however, sometimes I seem to feel it sink along the horizon lacerated with red
And orange wounds – is this where I'll meet
My mother this time, or myself, if I'm not careful

I walk up West Street aimlessly
With a cold stoicism and openness to possibilities
That I'm not unused to – but, I wonder:
How is this trail different from Piccadilly
Or Kioicho-dori, against which I ran with a red comet
Inside my womb towards the light rain at dusk –
With tremulous breaths – the perpetual earthquake of my Imperial Palace

Yet today I must be the furthest from Tokyo I've ever been
Closest to Antarctica, and its frigid rule of law
It feels like just yesterday I sat for my portrait, violets

In my hair, hope steaming in my veins, naked yet white hot in my diaphanous dress of ivory

No – this version of life – it isn't enough

When travel ceases – I work the graveyard shift for not one but two

Lives. The rush of silence fills the sweet, deep throats of this 56th floor aquarium which I now call home

So, the fish swim, the Ukranian war rages on, and I make chia pudding

Useless, glittering like the dark face of the moon. I watch the Fed

Hike rates as I turn up the *Grateful Dead*, but I cannot turn

Off the darkness. The antidote to reality is not escape, or dreams, but the passage of grief, surging and

Falling – yet I still wait for humans to go stay at the Mars hotel

And if this were the end of our Climate, I want only a balcony of white roses, Sylvia Plath poems to spend

Forever to read, and the chance to ask for a new planet to be from

Criminalized like red placenta, my thorny personality still chafes against the palette of the many

But I've ridden a riptide far and long enough

To look up and contemplate God – how I'm not like him when he eats me like Jesus

FRENCH RESTAURANT

Is it the ocean you hear in me? Its mercuric endlessness

Now I see the places and people that build me up, twenty-eight-feet tall, just to tear me down

Lay my head down in a hotel or an alien spaceship. I do not fear it. I've been

To heaven – where the stars plummet to their just address – my most earnest arteries

Girl From The Pale Blue Dot

I'm back at Café Kitsuné again, this time, comfortable
With the colossus of my past –
I ride the 1 train passing by Canal Street,
Then Houston – while the phone screens around me, like in a cinema,
Are lit up with the minute vicissitudes
Of our silent voyage

'An espresso for Gavin', screamed the pink-haired barista
Now words grow gelatinous – to create a new Constitution
They are no longer enough
On Charles Street a new family eat and speak about the war at my old dining table
I pick up my last few letters and packages, and I'm like –
When will it be my turn to forward them to Mars?

You ring me from California
I put on my new furniture and the clouds –
There's a girl who still likes the song that goes 'Once I wanted to be the greatest'
You say of course you know – we talk about the constitution of nostalgia, new food
recipes, getting direct sunlight, and my

FRENCH RESTAURANT

Annus horribilis. You ask, is this frigid sky capsule home that I built for a new start
Increasingly my heart

The news flash on my phone casually – did you know
That pulling out of the climate alliance is Vanguard?
That he is writing the next best English novel, or not –
It doesn't even matter, you see – all fiction is good fiction when it makes your voice break
In this life we are still in need of thunder and rain on some foreign boulevard

A black cat in the street corner tells me she's not afraid of losing
Her hair when she looks at the portrait I drew of her one day at age 33 and 45
She insists I'm as she is, like Voyager – in need of only a bouquet of flowers, a journal, and a view of the stars
I say, throw in a mini-fridge, please – let me have it as my night- and daylight, and a portal
To the future and the past
With my foot off the gas now, little girl, Goodbye until Andromeda

J.w.m. Turner

Spring, the one in me with wilted cherry blossoms, comes as you bring me a book
Named *Pulse* – it is my funny failure, I say
Holding up this mirror, in which you
Look back at me like a far sea with history, thick as blue gravy
You are no more a child than the sky is bored on this April afternoon – you stand
With a knot in your stomach as you loosen your shoes

In the morning in West London, my father was just a man
I now eat men like him
For breakfast – a restless train runs
Over his body, and he is out of view like smoke, while on a far shore horses
With a terrible hardness lay down to die
I consort with angels – drumming up and down his bones

I was a woman once upon a white cliff or two
I'm tired of reading my mother's travel journals – I've walked through cities, and then miles of
News that lately make me blue

FRENCH RESTAURANT

Without a map – or as the French say – a "plan"
I am almost
Someone going homewards to you

It's Lonely To Be On Earth Now

It's lonely to be on Earth now – do you know that Major?
Building this ship of fools to escape to Mars
The fluorescent light in meeting rooms draws on my inflammation
in this lone star state, underneath which I spin
in flashbacks when you were humming Suzanne
the day I left you, until the captain announced we were making
our descent into this tapestry of arteries made of lights
and love that goes missing

In my dream I walk towards the green sea that crystallized these
learned and noble feelings
I stand on every balcony of every hotel room, the clouds glistening
Atop a burning sunset – but why do I now feel nothing
All I can think of is my fridge light – how it waits for me –
Looking at me when I was confounded by artificial boundaries
aboard a thousand different flights

Near the cliffs you discuss the lightness of eternity
I solemnly declare eternity bores me, at age 6

FRENCH RESTAURANT

It's a Bank Holiday – little poppies dance on my skirt and my lips
We eat and swirl at a picnic – you say today
I can have loads of chocolate sweeties
While my brother is making a big red balloon disappear
Into his little fist

Your face wrinkles and bulges before me like scenery
The machines beep – I think it sounds like singing
But I'm not a smile, daddy
I can't erase the darkness that envelops me
I travel in space like electromagnetic waves – I've been burning
on both ends, a woman without a home – what you wanted me to be
I rise, I fall – I have nothing, yet everything I wanted

My Future

One day Manhattan will submerge within me
My heart redolent of the vivacious past it carries
The beauty who is at once the beast
The little girl in the mirror at one with her womanly being
All within my suitcase and me, just the two of us
Racing up Queens
To fly to India, or somewhere else hot where the stars never fall asleep

In this new regime I will breathe differently
I will make, and comfortably take, until there are trees
Everywhere in my garden – and I will teach, though words are not enough –
They can form cities, until my eyes can see
More clearly than ever the beauty of deserts, and not of oases
Not because of what had been, but what is always to come
My happiness is like water – omnipresent, flowing like a consistent stream

The hours pass – and at the end of the realm of themes
I find a room of my own – because life is of the

particulars:

My Sylvia Plath and Virginia Woolf stacks, sundresses, and scattered paper with my writing

I forage and make bouquets of orange tulips

They blossom next to glass doors while my terrible eggplant burns in the oven

But it doesn't matter – I'm not even hungry

I prefer to dance to scratched records that skip

Under the stars the winds fray my nerves slightly

But I regain my composure as I listen to the leaves

I will keep looking for the remains

Of the earthly storms within me

And unlike Andromeda I won't wait for Perseus by the cliffs

I will listen to the voice in my head

Which all along had been my own under the sea

Georgia O'keeffe, Ms. Allergic To Cheese

Next to sleeping willows, I realize I may not be a storyteller
Plots and characters are stagnating, like joint pain
I know not how to weave or untangle webs of interconnected words, last July or another
And punctuations, as my orange typewriter
Runs out of black ink

But in the afternoons, I forget about the hardship of barely
Walking up Bleecker and passing by Sullivan Street, and of not knowing you
So, I swallow whole a ham with French Dijon baguette sandwich
You're getting older, aren't you, in the street corner of my mind
And when the sandwich gets spicier in taste – should I keep it a secret or tell you?

The October wind passes through me, or is it the other way around?
When I think about the little Daikanyama hills, your steadfast shadow

FRENCH RESTAURANT

Under a building of four closed restaurants – later I knew it was a National holiday

This is far from the only story up my sleeve, but I want to write about it

And to tell you, I had gone back there to buy a white suitcase to carry my dresses and poems

But I'm out of pretty words, or

Connectors that make prose into song

I have only red bricks, grey walls of the architecture of my honesty

Facts – the dusk light of the night, of everywhere, for they are really the same

The weightlessness of me and of Fall

If I were only honest, I had never within

Me more than a meter of greenery

I stood up trees, and then forests, for you – and decorated the brick walls with pictures – as normal people do

Now I live with the remnants of a revolution

I read the Marxist Terms of Service, my head next to my species being when I cannot sleep

I bury you in the quotidian flickering of lights – traffic noises near the water – and digital copies of the FT

In the oven my dying green plant is marinating with my last boy's shaving cream

I once said – less is not more, yet less is enough

Well, that's what happens when you give a twenty-something the weight of thirty-something's

Most of the days I'm a stream-of-consciousness Georgia O'Keeffe – I'll build a wall and cut it down daily with the ones who quietly comprehend my inner scream

The girl next to me in the waiting room said she'll call her mother when the sun sets

I'll google what that means –

As a schoolgirl I never had packed lunches, and now as a woman I live without a piano, and my apartment is a Nietzschean mess

There are thoughts you can't clean but that's alright – I no longer live with the imminence of a mining disaster

A hotel room is where I belong – says Google Translate this fine morning

Ted Hughes

On the far side of the moon, my river Thames
Flows into yours, but the tides are teal and run smooth
With philosophical truths –
That of small rocks, and of the sky reticent in the rain
Whose horizon bleeds, but speaks to me in allegory
Like a fisherman that comes home with his nets
Wide and wet, and says –
The last star on your dress, responsible for Mars' first sunset

In this vivid dream I am braver at night
We jump into a chapter
That tastes like salted grains in a desert
Somewhere far but boisterous – a gravestone without willows
To strangle me with distasteful 'truths'
Alas, perhaps I have not met my Ted Hughes
Or have I – twelve or more years ago –
When the equator was a straight line that swallowed my continent whole

I throw my sneakers, sundress, and a lemon tart
into a washing machine, followed by an ossified ventricle of my heart

I wait for a thunderstorm to swallow the past in a flood
For lightning to hit me as your warning does
You dive into my marrow
with the ease of eating an apple
In your words I am at once my reflection in the sea
And a new character on Piccadilly unbeknownst to me

Youth

Summer streets come flooded with young, blonde girls in white tennis shoes
Reminds me of my mother when she was younger, crisper, but harboring more truth
My hair, however – it is a lot darker –
and my heart, too, with a palpitation that rings deeper
than the canonical verses that decorate the contours of youth on another day in June

She said he threatened to leave when she screamed in Calcutta under the moon
A silence envelops me, develops me – all that was misconstrued in the monsoon
No, I can't help now but wonder –
did she simply get sick of her jewels or run out of sandpaper
on which to fictionize him, "Mr. Win to Lose"

I wait anxiously for the crimson waves to bring me the news
At night they rush into my brain – my being and spirit washed away like the fake sand dunes
I built that year when I was smaller, where the sun looked brighter, and I didn't yet know my brother
I'm on that beach again but does it matter – in your novel

you made me better

I still long for the West African coast but hunt for a moment of rest before boarding another Ship of Fools

In my most poetic dream, we check into the only hotel on Mars and dance in my room

filled with white hydrangeas – we go fly fishing in Utopia Planitia, you say I have the wrong tools

For you are my witness, tell me I need not forgiveness and safeguard what remains of my tenderness

I could leave everything on Earth behind, even their verdict and my solitude

I still don't know how long a moment is, but I will travel to where only the sunset is blue

So Long, Ms. First Aid

I've been listening to the same damn song for ten damn days
You asked me for a clean slate – and if spring had taken shape
In New York the way I had said I wanted – on which lies my own face
with no trace of the past – the sordid, say, the Met Museum – effaced, set ablaze

When I met you, I was a womanchild who swindled in the art of being away
In my ear resounded the waves, and the frailty of being brave on a constantly emptying stage
On the phone my mother retorted, "of needing to go, but choosing to stay"
I think I believed her as I got taller – so I placed my hand on desolate moors as the earth quaked

I'm on the run, still, I paused in the waiting room when your blood stained my pillowcase
And like you, I break down then fashion the seasons into a new statue, despite the Siege of Calais
We watched *Cathy Come Home*, but you have to go, I know, I know – you said not all was in vain
Yet you still fogged up the mirror in Union Square Café,

"don't say goodnight to the bad guy" – it was quite unlike Scarface

Is it too soon, or too late to replace the bullets in my gun case –

And paint a portrait of mid-May –

the imminence of the naked certainty yet abruptness of heatwaves

Lay me down softly, sing me a heartfelt lullaby – soon I'll draw up the license to shine from words in a one-woman parade

We've missed the forest for the trees from a young age

Here, and everywhere, when I look up at the moon I see his face

Weathered, now lined in pain

But perhaps you'll be right beside me, in a way, transmitting from the weathervane as I learn to escape the Escape of our Age

Betelgeuse, See You At Sunset

Could someone show me how
A play, or two, that need not flop
Against exotic landscapes chorus singers chanted "forget me now"
To stay, when you have left – is to be within, and do without

So, say, what are the odds
That I close my eyes and see only a field of white hollyhock
April raindrops, unlike earthquakes, hit me like polka dots
Disappearing onto the pavement before the aftershock

Leaping into a meteoric downpour from atop
Can I let myself stay tender as Georgia O'Keeffe or should I stop
Around my neck tightens Orion's belt – the tune that rushed into my chest mellows out
Is this a dream, or is it not?

Vague D'azur

(Azure Waves)

Perhaps one day I will stop listening to Phoebe Bridgers
Within me time goes faster – then slower
When I chase it – the truth comes closer, then further
The night falls, I try to make sense of it all –
The Martian light grows only darker
where Ulysses sails the metaphorical water –
"Were you just another wild guess for the Tokyo reporter?"
Until the sun sets in Gibraltar, be a page-turning thriller
fading into the ether
I'm still the blower's daughter

風の歌を聴け

(Hear The Wind Sing)

Thomas called from Cannes one afternoon and said he's living on his boat, and something

half-ridiculous like "onwards to Africa, my banjo & your typewriter, no more blues"

For the second time that week in a drugstore lane I caught myself laughing

and pictured Paul Weller on a Citibike humming *My Ever-Changing Moods*

See, you think I'm Jo March, not "Sylvia Plath with her *Bell Jar*", living without gravity

But I – I turned the corner and almost forgot our bet about the next best Bombay monsoon

Three or four songs repeating in a loop on the interstate

I wanted to say I know you, and it's not too late, or too early to write a brand-new tune

But when the moment came I hesitated,

because I'm a liar, and I'm unsure how to interrogate the absurdist facets of our youth

and how I think I could go anywhere with him, even home, though perhaps I didn't want to – and in the dark you kept asking

has it been an eternity, at the movies, or a moment since we were twenty-two

You say it's ok if I change my mind again and move across the world, and collide

with satellites that are bound to find and miss a winter harvest moon

I saw you through the window that day – and I felt something – like passing flights

that glide through the skies, because I want to be consumed by a relentless storm in June

and wake in every extra-ordinary morning to a Schopenhauerian light – that of the depth of night

My father once told me nothing solid ever melts into air or fades from view

At the departure gate he kept saying he'd come with, and that's not what I wanted to hear

Though in a way it's what I always want to hear, but I don't want the stillness on the roof, or to be your Waterloo

25 felt like hallucinating, elated, out of air

Travelling in technicolor mists, to find an avalanche, or a breakthrough

And when I'm with her again in the chalet, dancing to French tunes I can't bear

We run out of vermouth, and she says it's time I fell from the news into the truth

FRENCH RESTAURANT

Because one night when the traffic light turned red you asked me to stop swimming

against the tide and stay, if I could, in Xanadu

But I was an acrobat, a diplomat who followed my head, left you a note saying nothing

except that I shall see you again when all is golden in hue

And I haven't left your mind since

An excuse – tabooed – a ruse – I'll be breaking all your countrymen's rules

Dancing With Father John Misty #2

In 2019 we were young enough to know everything

My guns were blazing

across Europe, and Tokyo drifting

Chasing a singular ideology I still look for silent planets that are burning

through an eternity

The waves were rising, and you say, now we're in the business of living

The sun – it also rises in the East

But men still perish in India, and some near Westminster Abbey

In a different galaxy

I traversed planets, consumed happily in a Leviathan tyranny

where the neon lights shone all night, layers of reality unfolding

in a rose-colored symphony – where I was one, and many, but never every

But summer, all wavered and bent against my home – the totality of New York City

Except "home" rang in my ears like an unspoken scream,

gone from its normalcy

The adults kept talking,

but you wouldn't stop bleeding

So we flew – far – where I asked the lion in Trafalgar Square, seen

once and for ever, for a prescription – a sense of meaning

Sometimes we roll down the blinds and wait for Life to hit us like lightning

Burn through the noise, leave only the truth – the best of me – the contours of my insanity, the ugly

The architecture of love is one of fluidity, like our youth, everchanging, fleeting

I put away your fragile verses in a carry-on for a trip to Mercury

Where the war is over if you choose, nothing to fear or lose – our hearts on our sleeves

The music in you, never-ending

Sweet As Summer, Then Sweeter

You wrote me a poem called summer
Running across the red poppy field I get wet and go skinny dipping in the river
Did you know at midnight it runs backwards?
Unlike time, kissing gladiators in St Germain and Westminster – now a new era on Bleecker

I always put on Michel Legrand when the stars grow dimmer
Sinking into a Godardian anarchy on apricot-stained writing paper
The waves surge in my mind & the boat catches on fire as we reached Martha's Vineyard
I dance to *That I Miss You* until we collide with a Sputnik sweetheart – a wonder, I wonder

They say I'm good at being brave – still, it rains – sometimes I get so tired of it I leave things scattered
So knock on my door with the Truth, disarm me like an easy-rider
Come as a devout Humbert Humbert, or a tenacious sailor – not a Knight in Shining whatever
Make me into something as sweet as summer, then

sweeter

Dream A Dream, Here's A Scene

In my dream you are never thirty
Running along the beach whispering Sexton's poetry, you laugh and call me a "wild thing"
The clouds gather with a sense of urgency – I am glad it masks my hesitancy and melancholy
I say, "I fought against the current", flying to New York in a heartbeat

But change, how it grounds me and then confounds me
The undercurrent of the past, humming with a dream-like quality
Caught in a seismic shift, no longer who I used to be
When I thought yesterday was forever, but forever is thirteen hours away – a Tokyo film scene, sans sous-titre

In a floral robe portefeuille I bathe in a new beginning
Red townhouses and carefree al fresco dining – yet do they harbor what I desire, the sense of uncertainty?
Out of the blue I catch a glimpse of imperial palace in the rain, the lights of Marunouchi, Ibaraki earthquakes in my sleep
Till the sun pours into my window and wakes me from an alternate reality – tell me, will I one day be missing Charles Street, so intensely?

The Greatest

We embrace in Akasaka,
a pallid silence crowds us
Say, you will remember the Fitzgeraldian parties
we peopled at twelve, half past
When you speak, you speak so substantially,
about your venture inwards, and towards Altair, Deneb, and Vega
Vowels and consonants – will you miss us – as roses miss white hydrangeas –
seized in an Archimedean coup d'état

Traversing through the world with a wilderness in my heart,
a festival of cinematic yet quotidian imprints, details that last
Out of the many women growing in me I seek to make one,
a dance I'm learning to choreograph
In which I also make love to your quintessence – yet this, too, shall pass?
– so indivisibly, in the style of Simone de Beauvoir
Yes, some people are in love
some yearn for the waves at night, driving towards which in a car

"I'm a big girl", I said, so I did not tear up as I leapt off Tokyo Tower, but smiled

at our meta-modernism, on your behalf

Yet what is the past

if not what is unsaid – "don't leave – I just need a wake-up call" – a song you'd better not grasp

The moon is rising, the stars are burning, as the skyline falls in a basement Shinjuku jazz bar,

my heart both near and far

Happiness is a butterfly in August on a Newport morning, the sunlight harsh

Against the waters of my nostalgia I set sail – towards the thundering storm in your heart of hearts

CHAPTER 2: TOKYO

Tokyo, Mon Amour

The sun rises in the east this time – unapologetic,
Like me. I wake up to a Tokyo oasis, punctuated by storied buildings
The contour of Mt. Fuji dances on the horizon – it speaks to me
Only in allegories – I think we are as close as we've been
In whirlpools I swim and look at clouds that remind me of the life I once gave away

Time passes as I resist the birth of this new poem
And its multitude of meanings, as sceneries and streets
Crystallize within me – I'll be in trouble if I let the physicality of Tokyo Tower enter my body
I walk abreast friends in Roppongi or Shinjuku, but I am my own blue shadow
Under the moon, I silence the sirens – I keep up this charade

How again after years there is the survival of details
And the feelings that encase the next best Tokyo earthquake – it has yet to arrive
Like my best poem. I live to be an archeologist to excavate the portion of life that takes place commensurate to our courage
No, I am not better at 'living' than I was three years ago

FRENCH RESTAURANT

But I want to light up my dashboard to travel to the landscape at the end of me – to make my own way in the world

In a different universe, where the cherry blossoms
Bloom in the depth of summer under a violet Akasaka night sky
I am perhaps someone, with a grocery list in my hand
For fresh fruits and flowers, 8PM on a Tuesday
Walking homewards to you

Tokyo Belle De Jour

Falling in love
Is like humming *Crimson and Clover*
Dreaming of a brunette Catherine Deneuve
Climbing Mount Fuji in February without gloves

Akasaka nights, I bathe in silver stardust
We sway to the silence, frosted by winter illuminations in Ginza
Waking up to *Norman fucking Rockwell*, no makeup
You say less is not more, yet less is enough

Guilty until proven innocent, awaiting the judge
Your heart atop an ume branch, next to a white dove
Frontpage stories we do not discuss, oh, my blood
Drinking English Breakfast Tea at the noisy Tokyo American Club, à bout de souffle

After The After

The thought of him – it used to linger

Like the bruises on my knee, growing darker, but then fader

Running past the imperial palace, an antiquated love, as my sun sets in his rush hour

The Roppongi neon lights against a neon moon, November – details, now vague as intergalactic dark matter

I once could write about him in a poem without pause or erasure

I dove into the deep blue waters of the night – the stars shifted as I came up for air – looking into the mirror at a serial killer

Are you in love or in pain, asked no one, ever

I said, "but what's the worst that can happen to a girl who's already hurt"

In a dreamland, I set sail towards a new answer

Create a different world order, have gun will travel, lead me to a story that is not proper

In it I'm unopened by a simple song, a 7am croissant, a never-ending summer

Catch me on the flipside in Kokomo, the Beach Boys on airplane mode – the here and now is after the after

Le Grand Brouillard

In my heart there flickered a light called Central Park

Meandering were strawberry fields punctuated by middle eastern men at ice cream carts

When the future was as indivisible as sunsets on Fifth Avenue – a world not yet divided in half

But then came the current – our white boats foundered, lost in the reservoir

I think of New York most on moonless Saturdays, but like my lovers, they come and pass

Violence in Union Square, burning cars – flaming headlines that tear us apart

Our bodies once young and naked in the summer grass, now outgrowing chains that sought to define us

When does this chapter end, and where does the next one start?

Perhaps one never disentangles the mystery of love, whispered the dark surfer from Okinawa

When we thought lost were the stars, really, lost was us

The radio turned up on a scenic drive, *reste avec moi*

Imminent is the antichrist – a transvaluation – we are on the cusp

Scream

You stood tall in a dark suit, an attitude of "all or nothing"

A kiss, unhinged, that of the 18th century

The rush of uncertainties running in my bloodstream

I want something bizarro and bleak – 6am crows of Roppongi

A shattered glass – a whisper in your ear, *"je n'suis pas d'ici"*

Making love to an impermeable metamodernity, L'Impératrice on repeat

Villefranche-Sur-Mer

Say, can you fragment a fragmented heart

Sweet as vermouth, blessed with rage, the chamber of sadness ajar

Despite its scars, pretending to be brave in a postmodern Tokyo seminar

Surfing the Biarritz surge of my mind, as the skyline falls, like a shooting star

My sundress on the terrace, Serge Gainsbourg on repeat punctuated by Jacqueline François

Your suntanned fingers through my hair against a clementine-colored Villefranche – and the reckless chords on your guitar

Cold was the night, named desire was a streetcar, now all afar

On the cusp of such hope – sailing into the eye of the storm, despite warnings on the radar

Except the storm was within me – sitting next to him in a Fitzgeraldian bar, when I was once, then, truly in love

Ground Control To Major Golightly

You came to me in a manic pixie dream
Wearing the fabric of your subtleties
Laced with my imperfections, rainy nights in Roppongi
Ceaselessly, a heart of hearts, the taste is sweet as *Jules et Jim*

You think I'm beautiful – yet I'm not a prayer on your lips
But it is with words, dark notes, I cut deep into your skin
A play by Euripides, one of impossibility and blasphemy
Despite the daylight between us, you'd dance under my architecture of fluidity

Falling in love with me is a Ponzi scheme
But one day, when you ascend Mt. Fuji, think of me dearly
Imagine us kissing, the look on my face delicate, as we fall off the cliff
Away from this heartbreak city – into a restless sea

When November Comes, I Stop Counting The Days

Say, can you hear, the celestial soundtrack to your fluoxetine

Your vast epilogue, page 37, projected on my silver screen

The earth chills, and in her cheap thrills, you built

An island for the young, floating in tears of aquamarine

I dreamed of us, eyes downcast, on the cover of a dated nautical magazine

Deeply we submit, to the poetry of a libertine, and an old Cretan film scene

My twin peaks are softening, your violet hill is meandering

Setting sail against the wind, diving for pearls, one war to win

CHAPTER 3: LONDON

The Arrow

Back of any black cab
Or on the train aisle near you en route
to Bath – if I've killed one man, I've killed two

Now I see myself distill into
colors on every horizon
When the sun inevitably rises

everywhere, and you speak from within the dim lights
in all my fridges, but not from the stage on which
I stand and look for commas – red like placenta –

in your old poems – our years never stiffened like my ribs,
now bruised with winter frosts, for they taught me Hope
Lately I stare at ceilings for their ghosts in search of you,
waking up to my own

Because growing old
is a relentless yet sacred activity
I'm drawn to those who are ugly

and unafraid to see beneath
my riverbed of strength, on which I seek to become

a violet becoming – at ease with what sleeps within me

I've lost my mother's watch, but now I foam to golden collared waves

I have only the flowers on my dress, clamoring at the distinctive atrocity of sunsets

I rested my head at the eye of the cauldron as History tightened its

Bow
But this time, I
Am the arrow

Army Of Me

(i)

Autumn arrived overnight, I say offhandedly on Bleecker Street
We didn't grow up here – we know not the tree rings to escape this Halloween maze
We were only sixteen when we thought we could be anything, and now
We are no longer at the party
Where the moon song was playing as you unscrewed the stars in Knightsbridge
I hated touching my spleen with you standing close to me
I say, like the summer rain this changes everything

In oatmeal textured dreams, I pick up *Ulysses* and read
My test results through technicolor Tom Ford glasses – unworn but dirty
They said I'm running low on hemoglobin that produces empathy
But my labs read, allergic to hypocrisy; perhaps the weather in New York is not damp
Enough to carry the colossus of me
A cloud of seismic shifts
Momentous

FRENCH RESTAURANT

The zoologist in me told you
About the emerald green alewife swimming
In my kitchen sink –
the drain stopped working, the fish
Are poisoned with pea protein powder and old manuscripts
You didn't want to call in the bomb squad at 2am
So I turned up *Julia Jacklin* as I got on a plane and did not speak

(ii)

I walk from Mayfair towards the Embankment with answers
A hardline – I drew it myself this time
A storm is coming; I don't mind
A far sea moves in my ear and then towards my left ventricle – I am aware of my heart
The opening and closing of it, like doors
And the white doves, they may no longer sing
That's alright; I am letting them go, surly

In East Sussex, the mist hugs a setting sun above white cliffs like a canopy
No need for a hero in this sky – except for my words in the orange notebook
That I carry to cafes across oceans, towards another

Version of life – as the living of the old one fades from view

Like the brass waves next to Japanese akari bringing the past and future into sharper relief as they recede

My heels click on London pavements – but I'm made of warmth and salt like the sea

Will I ever see land again?

(iii)

I have come to know that the Tokyo earthquake alarms will forever ring in me

I came by those sceneries by accident, which may ossify into sculptures

But not my musings

Just as I know those days by the Prince Gallery

Will eventually fracture like my bones, and will scarcely come back to me

I preserve them, in silhouette and substance, until I find them again

Amidst the waves

But this poem, which punctuates time at the heart of me, delineates the war of my twenties and its myriad casualties

It may not even be a poem – do you see?

Just a handsomely lit Piccadilly of vowels and consonants

Tower Bridges of existentialist ideas – which flow through your arteries

Together with my lacerated, postmodern sentence structures on Squares of unequivocal candor –

Constitute this elaborate and now bare

Body of me

One Day

In high school you bring me withering bouquets on racing day

In love with his beat poetry, my white tennis shoes, living in a Belgravian horseplay

The sun coats the Surrey polo field with gold, a star and her Ricochet

My wild temper, a raging sea, burning through a postmodern European decay

Two suitcases in JFK, a heart in a getaway car racing down West Side Highway

Morningside Hegel debates – swerving was our ambition, yellow cabs, and the ballet

Sitting for my portrait, as time alters my face, when forever was yesterday

Yet yesterday was *Hiroshima, Mon Amour* – a lifetime away

So I sailed close to Victoria Harbor, or Tokyo Bay

Talking philosophy, with his, and his hands on my waist

Finding out how my lipstick tastes, short stories become ill-adapted plays

The hotel rooms went still as the stage, the future, without a trace

I'll fly back to Manhattan and color spring in black Gaultier

Drifting back to a prince who'd been waiting with my crown in Union Square Cafe

In a kingdom downtown, Jackson Pollock served with my morning soufflé

Making love on an ordinary Wednesday, elated by the heaviness of Mrs. Dalloway

And I'll wake up to clearer blue skies, while I lead you astray

Soft ice cream on my lips, a summer day, still I'd leave you for Johannesburg or Bombay

You don't fall in love once, or twice, but a thousand times, until your heart is on display

An apocalyptic genesis with a dash of out-of-context sadness, my forté

CHAPTER 4: HONG KONG

The Life Before Us

Sunday afternoons – they no longer rush into my windows
Like waves – they are quieter these days, you say
And time, it can bend sideways – turns out I left morsels of me on different continents
Some I can only find again when I return to them
When it rained in New York yesterday
I picked up the phone and rang the travel agent
For a ticket to myself. She said, 'sold out for this week – for the one-way'

CNN is on, and I make chocolate baked oats as the knowledge
Of our mortality inundates me. I think of Chinese fish that can't swim
In the Pacific – they work as conductors on the transcontinental
Underwater subway, breathing in the dollars until the structural integrity
Of our trading framework disintegrates
For this is how being bi-cultural punishes us –
We are privy to the hypocrisy of our personal history and that of our nation states

Now I'm finally on this flight – you'll be there when I land, but if not, that's ok
The runway is cleared for takeoff, unlike my brain
I watch the seatbelt sign go on and off in the hanging gardens of
Babylon. The pilot asks on the radio as they serve us fisheye gel with caviar
'Is life sad but beautiful, or beautiful but sad?' So I thought, does it matter anyway
If I were heading to Hong Kong, New York, or outer space?
Will there be photos of me and my mother in my room tonight and when I hit replay?

And that one day I will learn that there is time, and then its malleability
It is what tethers me to the ground – my mother and motherland, my flesh and blood
– Yet it also sends me to impossible summits. A train
Thunders across the mountain ridge, mating as they give birth, shrieking
The equator encircles us and readies itself to be our God
Time ticks and licks my inner wrist as the river carries us home in its rambunctiousness
I'm youthful and ancient, all at once, in the crepuscular womb of daybreak

Souvenir

My love, I said, take me to the lights
In your eyes, dictated by silent planets of the night
Diseased with sadness, but with a vision, we stood under the tall elm trees
With a prescription, you were Edwardian, and erudite

Time was moving, through you, against a pallid grey sky
Aged and faded, summer evenings and our fluorescent gunfights
The waves were rising, and now we are living
And commemorate you will, our most ordinary, Sunday morning stage fright

Hunter S. Thompson

You wrote three lines of poetry, painted me blue
Pierced through my thoughts, and our sonorous tune
The silhouette of my existence, searching for the roses on my dress upon my bed
Driving in your car, The Beach Boys, wandering down the avenue

I said, be wild, but fear the war I'm waging inside of you
A novel from start to finish, we paced, and around us, violet fumes
But happiness, it comes in waves, like the way you tune the radio
Till the coastline grows obscure, one song to choose

CHAPTER 5: PARIS, ROME, ZERMATT, TASMANIA, TORONTO

Around The World In 365 Days

Wake up anywhere, I used to see him in textured dreams
I could say I remember his kiss, sweet like soft ice cream
But I don't, for he's only the remains of a vanilla day
Called summer, Eastbourne by the sea
But it is an abundant winter night now, and I walk down
Piccadilly towards you
Opening up
Like my unadorned black dress for New Year's Eve
At the seams

I take off and touch down, stranded in reveries
Some sixty-four times this past year, forgetting old sceneries
By the window, or the aisle
Always running towards a fire, away from a story
When my heart was dithering, into which you were looking
But some people only looked
Into my eyes
So singularly. No more New York tap-washed cherries
Or Central Park, saccharine fields of strawberries

So I will eat a cornetto al prosciutto and throw all my shirts, silk

FRENCH RESTAURANT

Into the sea, no restaurants or clubs, just white daffodils

By the kitchen sink, you'll take off my armor, East Liberty St or Yorkville

We'll toast to the petty fragments of life, and my piano-playing, very ill

And you'll hold me close, say you want time to slow

And never goodbye, even when we

Run out of words, or when your tears run down my Achilles heel

Standing still, no wine to spill

Until my heart sinks no longer, as I run up that hill

Sweet Clementine, Run Away With Me

'Sweet Clementine run away with me'

I whisper calamitous news into your ear in front of a Konrad Witz painting

You contemplate the constitution of our modernity –

It is just not enough to follow the script. You drive the getaway car and yell "get in"

The siren blasts as we plunge into the lake, coming up for air, "naturally,

I say, "we'll sing Silent Night in C-minor on this Apocalyptic Christmas Eve"

I run as I do – but when the moon rises, we meet in the dark corners of your illicit dreams

A totality of impossibilities – what if's – all dissipating

into an ill-starred franchise of Henry James stories

Shall I hang on the edge of a feeling, eyes red like those glistening atop Tokyo buildings

Or play tennis afield a tree-lined court in a dialectical tragedy-comedy – the clock strikes 14h14 in Mozambique

Do you know I'm still just like you – unafraid, strange, and crazy?

The Queen of Capulet at dawn, windows down, a New York grocery run dressed in

uncertainties – with which she'll find a new continent to lie down and get up on the daily

Will it strengthen you if I showed you the face of my landslide victory

A French thriller of Shakespearean intensity

An art heist trialed for its duality – surf a fluorescent climax, then a comedown multiplying in intensity

In the Geneva deposition I said, "I merely clapped for the pantomime"

Unstructured St. Germain Musings #2

The sun comes up, half mad – but this time
It ripples in a Giverny garden –
Strangely, Italian crudo dance on delicate plates and sing
Their swan song at lunch in St. Germain
As panorama cameras linger
On waterlilies, and then upon my overwhelmed esophagus

When night falls, I undress and swim quietly in an impressionist stream
Men in Le Marais sporting white turtlenecks speak to me
In Egyptian riddles – their notes rise only higher
I stand next to a little red door and decline
to dance to the tune of their meta-modernity
For who doesn't have the blues? A pan-communist Sphinx

The lights upon the Seine traversed across time, wars,
And notions of democracy to find me
And my foreword in the same metaphysical symphony
You see – it isn't a play this time I want to write – nor is it a paper
About "digital" trends – discard them along with my old,

saccharine

Self, please – I want and to be a Fauvist dream, of the palpable daily

The silhouette of this night takes shape

At last - *all that is solid melts into air* in St. Germain, which agrees with me

Perhaps what I want so hard to say is that

Those who came before us simply abducted a sense of precocious disenchantment

From within our sleep. On the other side of the Atlantic

Young women forage, make wreaths, and retain their creativity, even against the sordid West Village breeze

CHAPTER 6: CALIFORNIA & ARIZONA

The Night Symphony

A rtemis, guide me now, in this time of unrest –
For I walk on unfamiliar roads charred by crimson twilight, advancing towards
Or is it away from the Sun
I have not picked up the pen for ages, beset by sentence structures of mediocrity
Architected to fissure those with imagination into syllables
In my dream you wrote to me out of the blue as the moon waned
I hadn't forgotten how to write about it – elation or sadness taken out of context

The Arizona mountainscape overwhelms me with notions
Of disparate lived realities – I am here, aren't I? From Sedona to the Grand Canyon
The scenic train traverses through greatness of a particular kind
I am unable to name it. I search for a vision
Of God in our rearview mirror, how she laughs at eons of pain
My vision blears as I have a shuddering thought about interest rates – so I pull up the FT
As we lunch at the local café in town, apologetic about

asking for almond milk towards the waitress

At the edge of the Canyon, or is it under the sweeping, starry night sky

Ursa Major comes down to the plains to tell me a bedtime story

About when the town is silent, how he wants to die, and how death starts like

A dream, full of objects and the drumming on of desert winds

I ask if he wants a slice of shepherd's pie made with cactus

His eyes glimmer like glazed, yellow marbles but says –

'We are at war with Orion, and soon they'll ration meat pies in this galaxy'

Spacetime warps and brings me back to an insoluble evening at Monkey Bar

Not far from where we worked together and where buildings aged slowly like trees

He said 'the tectonic plates shift at night' as pink clouds of mass delusion

Mantled the horizon line, eliding meaning

A storm raged within my spleen. I rushed to interpose something

Enduring between us and the insurgence of the quotidian

You see, I felt we struggled with the same thing – the danger of being 'old folks' at twenty-three

He crystallizes into a dot as I set my watch for the duration it takes to migrate from excitement

To apathy. I look up at the stars again, only this time, I see the portrait of our twenties –

How your eyes flicker

And your mouth moves to urge me to quit my job before Christmas Eve

Don't I know it – as if Anne Sexton could play by the rules

Now I will grow my own fruit. My face is calm as a mannered sea

I get off the Merry Go Around of this Earth, riding away from the extinction scene

AFTERWORD

One may understand the cosmos, but never the ego; the self is more distant than any star.

– G.K. Chesterton

ABOUT THE AUTHOR

Renee De La Roche-Zhu

Renee de la Roche-Zhu is a poet whose work draws from her global upbringing and diverse life experiences across academia and business. Her poetry explores the liminal spaces of existence, identity, and human connection, weaving the quotidian with the philosophical and transcending linear time. Renee graduated from Columbia University in the City of New York with a B.A. in Economics-Mathematics and Philosophy. Outside of poetry, Renee is a member of the startup community, having previously worked at the global management consultancy McKinsey & Company as an Associate Partner across North America, Asia, and Europe and as an analyst at Goldman Sachs in the Investment Banking group.

www.ingramcontent.com/pod-product-compliance
Lightning Source LLC
Chambersburg PA
CBHW051348040426
42453CB00007B/475